Drawing & Seeing

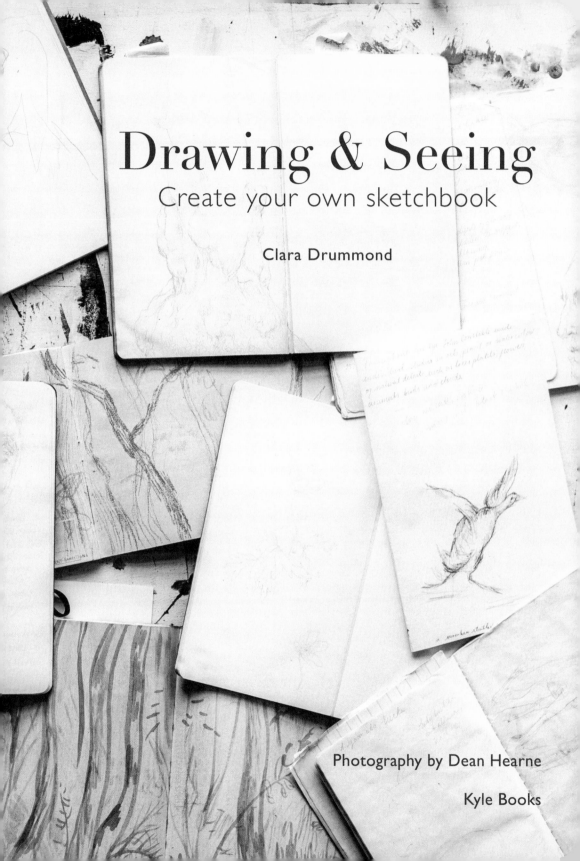

Drawing & Seeing
Create your own sketchbook

Clara Drummond

Photography by Dean Hearne

Kyle Books

Acknowledgements

I would like to thank HRH the Prince of Wales and Catherine Goodman for founding the Royal Drawing School, a rare and inspiring place that nurtures individual talent and has supported hundreds of young artists since it opened in 2000. I will always be grateful to the School for everything that it has taught me about drawing and being an artist.

Daphne and Micky Astor for their wisdom, encouragement and great kindness.

My husband, Charles Gouldsbrough, for all the happy hours we have spent drawing together and for helping me with so many elements of this book.

My mother and father to whom I owe so much and who are the reason that I became an artist.

I would also like to thank my editor, Sophie Allen, for all the hard work and patience that brought this book into being, and Peter Blake, Chrissy Blake, Paula Rego and Jackie Honsig-Erlenburg for their generous contributions to this book and artists Anna Ilsley, Tamara MacArthur and Theodore James for drawing with me and for their feedback, and Maggie Hanbury for her guidance and advice. I am particularly thankful to Jonathan Yeo for being a wonderful friend and mentor, David Ross for his support and for believing in me from the beginning, Nicholas Cullinan, Christopher Baker, Jenny Saville, Sarah Howgate, Alan Hollinghurst and Des Volaris for selecting my portrait of Kirsty Buchanan for the first Prize in the BP Portrait Award and changing the course of my life.

An Hachette UK Company
www.hachette.co.uk

First published in Great Britain in 2018 by Kyle Books, an imprint of Kyle Cathie Ltd
Carmelite House
50 Victoria Embankment
London EC4Y 0DZ
www.kylebooks.co.uk

ISBN: 978 0 85783 4430
Text copyright 2018 © Clara Drummond
Design and layout copyright 2018 © Kyle Books

Distributed in the US by Hachette Book Group,
1290 Avenue of the Americas,
4th and 5th Floors, New York, NY 10104

Distributed in Canada by Canadian Manda Group,
664 Annette St., Toronto, Ontario, Canada M6S 2C8

Clara Drummond is hereby identified as the author of this work in accordance with Section 77 of the Copyright, Designs and Patents Act 1988.

Designer: Tina Smith Hobson
Photographer: Dean Hearne
Stylist: Jeska Hearne
Project Editor: Sophie Allen
Editorial Assistant: Sarah Kyle
Production: Lisa Pinnell

A Cataloguing in Publication record for this title is available from the British Library

Printed and bound in China

10 9 8 7 6 5 4 3 2 1

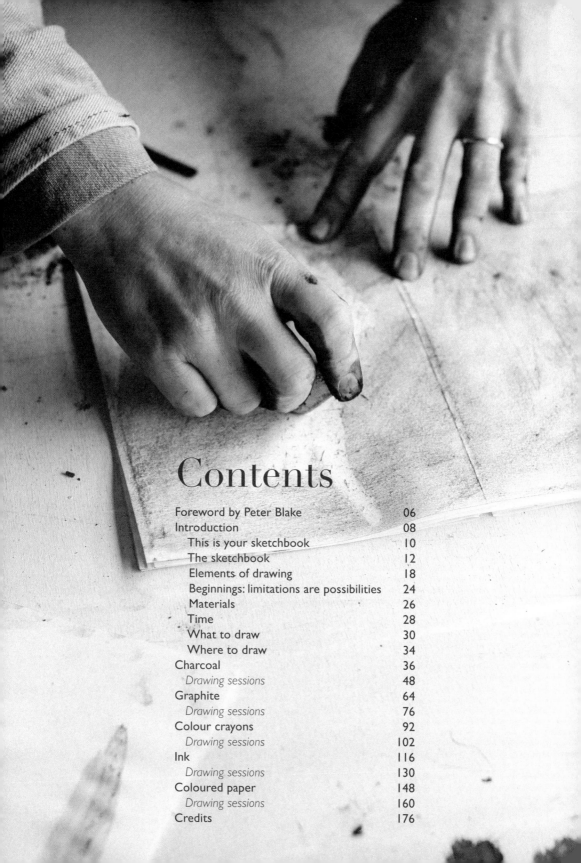

Contents

Foreword

As a young art student, I was taught to always carry a sketchbook. I have carried one ever since, for more than seventy years. I was Professor of Drawing at the Royal Academy Schools and, as a teacher, at that time, there would have been little chance of persuading the students to draw. Instead, I arranged a series of lectures by master draughtsmen, like Colin Self and others. I arranged visits to my studio where I showed them drawings by artists like Stanley Spencer and David Hockney.

The students were given a gift bag containing a little drawing by me, a sketchbook, pencil, pencil sharpener, an eraser and sometimes a chocolate pencil.

My hope was that this would encourage the students to use a sketchbook every day. My advice today is the same – carry and use your sketchbook.

Peter Blake

→   Peter Blake, 'Two stones which Liberty found on the beach, and gave to me to draw' pencil on paper, 'Paper Parasols, Hospitalfield House, Arbroath, Scotland', ink and crayon on paper, from the Scottish Sketchbook, 1976

③

INTRODUCTION

Drawing from observation is a process of discovery, a process that makes you discard your preconceived ideas of how things are and instead leads you to look to see how they really are.

'A moment, intensely seen and intensely felt…' is how the French painter Pierre Bonnard described the two-minute drawings that he made in his small pocket diary each day. In these swift drawings everything is seen as if for the first time: the weather, people, objects, interiors, landscapes and their texture and tone. He transforms the experience of seeing these daily sights into vivid records of a moment lived.

The best way to learn about drawing is simply to draw and to draw often. Like our response to colour, drawing what you see is very subjective. The great artist and teacher Joseph Albers, author of *Interaction of Colour* (an experimental way of studying and teaching colour), placed practice before theory. He said, 'Knowledge and its application is not our aim: instead it is flexible imagination, discovery, invention…'

Likewise, sketchbooks have long been a valuable tool for artists to do this, a place to capture the particular, the fugitive, the marvellous and the mundane. They continue to be a vessel for the genesis of ideas, for collecting influences and inspirations, a place where drawings can evolve, be kept safe to be transformed into other works or not, a place to capture what we see and how we see it. A sketchbook can be a record of a journey, or a sort of visual diary.

Whatever form a sketchbook takes – be it some bits of paper bound together, an ordinary notebook or a diary – it is portable and so gives us the freedom to draw anywhere. From Antonio Pisanello drawing animals in the wild to Ludwig Kirchner drawing in the crowded streets of Berlin, sketchbooks give artists the autonomy to experience the world first hand.

The materials that you will need for this sketchbook are:
- Several pieces of medium-sized charcoal
- 4B–8B graphite pencil or graphite stick
- Coloured wax crayons
- Bottle of Indian ink
- Chalk
- Medium-sized watercolour brush
- Fixative

And you will also need a watercolour brush, a jam jar, some rags or kitchen paper.

← Lucian Freud (1922-2011), Bedroom with Stolen Socks, 1940, ink on paper

This is your sketchbook

This is a book about keeping your own sketchbook, a drawn diary of your daily life and what strikes you. The pages are for you to fill, make a mess, take risks, try things out, to be fearless and to be curious, but most of all to look and to respond to what you see.

Along the way, there are suggestions about materials you might use and things you might want to consider while you are drawing, but they are there as a guide rather than as a rule.

There is space for 30 days of drawing; you can do them in whichever order you like. If you make a drawing that you are not happy with, don't be hard on yourself or rub it out – no one can really judge their own drawings until days, weeks or even years after they have made them. The most important thing is not that the drawings are all a success, but that you take a moment to pause each day, or as often as possible, to look and to draw.

By the time you reach the last page I hope that you feel that you can draw wherever you are, that you don't need a studio or all the time in the world, but that with the simplest of materials and some paper you can experience how drawing transforms the way you see.

'Everywhere I looked, nature was alive, in the sky, in the clouds, atop every stone, and between the branches of the trees — everywhere lived and stirred my wild and lively creatures, clamouring to be put in my sketchbook...'
Emile Nolde, 1867–1956

→ Charlotte Salomon (1917-1943), Self-portrait, Villefranche-sur-Mer, 1939-1941, crayon on paper (38.7 × 20cm)

The sketchbook

The sketchbooks that survive intact give us a precious insight into the work, lives and feelings of the artists who made them, sometimes across hundreds of years. We can see how, through frequent use, a unique drawing language emerges and an artistic identity is formed.

One of the oldest known surviving sketchbooks in Europe was made by a Frenchman called Villard de Honnecourt. It contains 33 pages of parchment haphazardly bound together. All that we know of Honnecourt is what can be discovered from this sketchbook. Thought to have been made between 1225 and 1250, during his travels in France and Hungary, it is characterised by an intellectual curiosity and a freshness of vision. He drew mainly ecclesiastical buildings and architectural details, but dotted among the pages there are also drawings of many strange and startling things, such as a snail with four antennae, a labyrinth, a knight, two parrots, a viol player with a dancing dog, a lion tamer, a wild hare, as well as studies of people and inventions such as a machine of perpetual motion and a copper hand-warmer. The slightly wooden style of his drawing is not unusual for his time as artists often copied from pre-existing images. What is surprising is that many have been drawn from direct observation. He even writes clearly next to a drawing of a large lion, 'Here is a lion seen from the front. Please remember that he was drawn from life.'

There has been much debate over the original purpose of this sketchbook, but it is now generally thought to have been a pattern or model book.

'Seeing a drawing is like taking the back off a clock and seeing all the little wheels spinning round and understanding how it works.'

Lucian Freud, 1922–2011

The origin of the modern-day sketchbook can be traced back to such medieval 'pattern books' or 'model books'. Artists used these bound collections of drawings as a sort of archive of subjects and motifs from various places to be used at a future point in paintings and illuminated manuscripts. The books were generally used by artists' workshops rather than by individual artists, and were passed on from generation to generation and from workshop to workshop. The highly finished pen and ink drawings that they contained frequently depicted natural forms, such as birds, plants and animals, which were mainly copied from other existing works of art. Many of the finest model books were made in Lombardy, Italy. The most impressive of those that survive can still be seen in the Biblioteca Civica in Bergamo, Italy.

2389

Much of what we know about how artists worked during 1300–1400 is thanks to the Florentine artist Cennino Cennini (c1370–c1440) who wrote *Il libro dell' arte* (*The Craftsman's Handbook*), a detailed description of the late medieval artist's workshop and techniques. He recommended that artists should draw from nature whenever possible, but at this time most artists still preferred to copy from model books. It was not until imaginative and explorative artists like Antonio Pisanello (1395–1455) that the model book tradition was transformed. He broke the mould with his spontaneous and inventive drawings of birds in flight and other creatures in motion made directly from life. Gradually, sketchbooks

↑ Samuel Palmer (1805-81) & Richmond, George (1809-96), Studies of Rabbits with superimposed portraits of William Blake and Henry Fussell, graphite and ink on paper

← Antonio Pisanello (1395-1455), Peacock and Six Monkeys, from The Vallardi Album, pen and ink on paper (b/w photo)

began to be used for a more expressive and experimental type of drawing. From the 1490s onwards, they tended to belong to individual artists as opposed to workshops, and so their function changed: no longer a standard workshop tool, but an artist's intimate possession, full of the character of its maker.

Ever since, the ways in which the sketchbook has been used are as varied and colourful as the practice of drawing itself. Paula Rego's sketchbooks are full of the workings out of compositions for her large-scale works. She draws from her imagination as well as from life, using models and props in her studio to explore the myriad of narratives that inspire her. Henri Gaudier Brzeska used the pages of his sketchbook to make drawings from life of animals and figures, which he then gradually abstracted in a series of drawings until he reached completely new forms.

William Turner used his sketchbook to capture the ephemeral effects of the weather and light as well as to record journeys that he made across Britain, Italy, Spain, France and Belgium. On every page a new landscape unfolds as

← Paula Rego, No. 31. Study for 'The Soldier's Daughter', Pencil on paper (42 x 29.5cm)

though we are travelling with him, seeing each new vista through his eyes. He would also use his sketchbook to take note of everyday things that interested him. On one journey home from Portsmouth he drew people ploughing and sowing, a woman cutting turnips and 'cows rambling among the furze'.

Henry Moore's famous 'Shelter sketchbooks' (page 154) are focused on civilians sheltering in the underground during the Blitz. Together, this series of drawings gives an overpowering sense of the feeling of being huddled together in the dark, and the sketchbooks become a window into another world.

For other artists, keeping a sketchbook is a way of not letting life slip by, such as Louise Bourgeois for whom drawing was a daily, almost obsessive, activity that recorded her emotions, her memories and her thoughts. She used ink, charcoal, crayon or whatever material came to hand. She once stated, 'I keep three kinds of diaries: the written, the spoken (into a tape recorder), and my drawing diary, which is the most important... They must be up to date so that I'm sure life does not pass me by... But the only diary that counts is the drawing diary'.

Peter Blake keeps two distinct sorts of sketchbook. He takes one with him on trips away or when he goes to see something in particular, like a circus; and another which is more private, in which he puts down thoughts and ideas. In the first type of sketchbook he nearly always makes a note of the time and the place where the drawing was made. He told me that when drawing in a sketchbook, 'You are quickly recording the interesting things about that day... they are a kind of memory aid... Sketchbook drawings trigger my memories and that's what it's about'.

Some 500 years earlier, this idea of a sketch-book as an aide-mémoire is suggested by

Leonardo da Vinci, '... Take pleasure in seeing and considering the actions of men... make a note of them with a few lines in your little book which you should always take with you... For these are not things to be erased but preserved with great care, because these forms and actions are so infinite in number that the memory is not capable of retaining them, wherefore keep your sketches as your aids and teachers'.

Francisco Goya, on the other hand, created a type of drawn journal. Unusually for the time, these drawings were descriptions of what he thought rather than what he saw. They were never intended to be exhibited. Each one gives form to Goya's feelings about the turbulent times in which he lived and his observations of human nature. They are often funny and sometimes tragic, but always piercingly honest. Each image is freely drawn and vividly alive, mainly made with ink wash or crayon. He made nearly 600 drawings, bound into eight albums, an extraordinary record of his incredible imagination and creative mind.

Another prodigious keeper of sketchbooks was Pablo Picasso. He even wrote, '*Je suis le cahier*' ('I am the sketchbook') on the cover of one, showing the extent to which he felt that it was an extension of his mind and hand, or possibly that he himself was a sort of human sketchbook collecting and storing images and ideas. He is known to have made 175 sketchbooks, and they reveal the arc of his creative process. Many of them show Picasso working through variations on a theme, using drawing as a means to experiment and play with visual ideas. His sketchbooks show that a freedom to play is vitally important for all forms of creative invention. As Grayson Perry says, 'Between the covers (of a sketchbook) I feel safe – the drawings need never be seen by anyone but me – and thus I can play.'

Elements of drawing

No drawing can be an exact transcription of what we see, but is instead a record of the experience of seeing, or more precisely how you see the world in that moment, on that day in the frame of mind that you are in. With each drawing, different elements may come to the fore, one drawing may be characterised by its texture and surface while another by its strong sense of depth, or by its scale or the way that it is placed on the page. However, it will probably be a combination of many things that gives it a power and life of its own. When you study drawing it can be useful to consider these different elements separately in order to better understand them. Once you have absorbed these lessons, you can 'forget' them in order to arrive at a means of personal expression. Pierre Bonnard recalls his experience of this moment of arrival in a conversation about his work with Raymond Cogniat:

'One day all the words and theories which formed the basis of our conversation – colour harmony, the relationship between line and tone, balance – seemed to have lost their abstract application and become concrete. In a flash I understood what I was looking for and how I would set about achieving it.'

This book focuses on various aspects of drawing. Here are just some of the elements that you will encounter in the course of filling these pages.

LIGHT
Light describes everything that we see; by depicting the areas of light and dark that you

'I can remember the precise moment when I realised that the shape of the picture gave it a great deal more power.'
David Hockney

observe you can create the illusion of form, volume and depth. Our perception of light is relative and everything appears to be either lighter or darker, depending on what surrounds it. Understanding tonal relationships and how to describe them is one of the most vital ways of exploring the full potential of drawing.

LINE
A line can express many things, so it is crucial to experiment with making different qualities of line: dark, light, broken, solid, fluid or choppy, smudged or precise – there is no end to the variations that can reflect the nature of your subject. To draw something as a simple line is sometimes the most direct and economical way of capturing the essence of what you see, especially if you are drawing quickly or drawing a moving subject.

MOVEMENT

It is rare for any living thing to ever be completely still and even when we are drawing something that is still, the process of seeing is an act of movement in itself. When drawing, it is important to find a means to translate movement into marks in order for your drawing to feel alive. Drawing at speed or drawing something that is moving swiftly can be a very good way of discovering ways of mark making that express a sense of movement.

SCALE

Lucian Freud used to say that an artist must amplify reality in order to capture how things really are. It is often the case that drawing on a small scale can diminish your subject, while drawing something on a larger scale can bring it to life. Filling your page and drawing off the edges can give a strong sense of life and energy. For these reasons, it is important to experiment with scale in your drawing in order to see the different effects it can have.

COMPOSITION

Within the edges of the page there is an infinite variety of possibilities to how you can place your drawing, and the way you choose to compose your drawing can change it dramatically. For example, by shifting the horizon line up or down, cropping or de-centering your drawing you can

← Pablo Picasso (1881-1973), Bulls and Lancers, 1959, in 'Toros y Toreros', published by le Cercle d'Art in 1961, ink on paper

create a more dynamic composition. One way to try out new compositions is to start your drawing in a different place to where you would normally, for example, draw from left to right, or from top to bottom.

TEXTURE
Texture is all around us; the surface of things is part of what makes up their character. A drawing can reflect this variety of sensation and touch with different marks: soft and hard, detailed or rough, fluid or jagged, fuzzy or clear. Experimenting with different materials, combining them in various ways or working on a prepared surface can create a lively and sometimes surprising surface.

DEPTH
You can create a believable space within your drawing by describing depth. The illusion of depth can be rendered in various ways. Using tone is one way as points of light can bring things forward, while areas of shadow can make them recede. You can also vary your mark within your drawing. The eye reads things that are closer to you with more clarity – so you can draw what is closer more boldly and in more detail than what is far away. Van Gogh used to draw the foreground with great attention, which gave his landscapes a strong sense of depth.

TRANSPARENCY and OPACITY
Varying the transparency or opacity of your mark can bring life, movement and depth to your drawing. This can be achieved by using different drawing materials – some are more transparent or opaque than others. Or you can dilute a material, such as ink, or vary the amount of pressure that you use with a material like graphite. When drawing in a transparent way you can create layers of marks on top of each other or you can draw opaquely over a transparent ground.

MEMORY
Our visual memory is an incredibly rich source of inspiration, both for working from the imagination and for drawing from observation. It informs how we see the world and how we choose to depict it. Like a muscle, the memory can be trained, so in this sketchbook there are several pages dedicated to simply looking, before drawing from memory. The more you use your memory to draw, the more effective it will become at retaining imagery and sensations.

COLOUR
Our reaction to colour is immediate and instinctive. For this reason, colour is often used to express feeling or sensation as opposed to being used in a descriptive way. Unlike form, colour is more personal so its interpretation is more open. Colour is relative; how we perceive it depends on what surrounds it. By placing colours opposite, such as orange and blue, yellow and purple, red and green, next to each other you can make them appear to 'pop'. Artists such as Van Gogh often used these strong contrasts to make their drawings and paintings vibrate with energy and light.

Beginning: limitations are possiblities

This sketchbook is divided into five sections, the first four focus on a drawing material, and the final chapter is dedicated to exploring different ways of combining them and the various papers that you can draw on. Some of the materials may be ones that you use rarely or not at all, and others may be ones that you use all the time. The purpose of dedicating each chapter to one of them is to create parameters and to encourage you to experiment within them.

Getting going is the priority and, in my experience, one of the obstacles to beginning a drawing, or any work of art, is having too many options: which material to use, how much time to spend on each drawing, what subject to choose, and so on. Parameters limit the number of decisions that you have to make before you begin, therefore helping to make the perfect conditions for creating. Inspiration follows action and not the other way round.

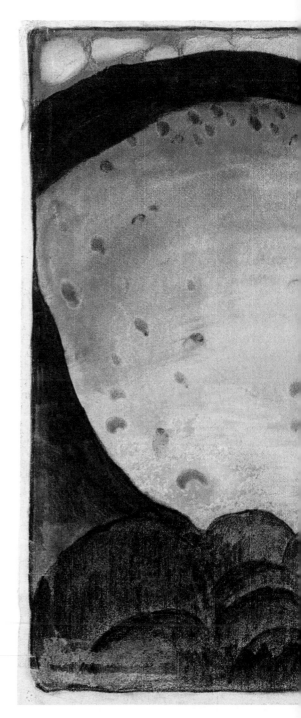

↓ Georgia O'Keeffe (1887-1986), Special no. 15, 1916; charcoal on off-white laid paper (47.9 × 61.9cm)

Materials

Much like sketchbooks themselves, drawing materials are very portable. With nothing more than a crayon in your pocket you are free to draw wherever you venture: in the street, in galleries, around your home and in the wilderness.

There is something very primal about using materials that we hold directly in our hand. The raw material becomes the tool and connects you to the first human who had the impulse to draw, carve or paint an image. Many drawing materials, such as charcoal and red chalk, are used in pretty much the same way now as they were 40,000 years ago. It is inspiring to think that these are perhaps the only materials that are still used in exactly the same way now as they were by our ancient ancestors.

The materials introduced in this sketchbook are inexpensive, easily obtainable and have never become obsolete. Like most drawing materials they are stable, permanent and simple; you can usually trust your instincts on how best to use them.

Drawing is an opportunity to respond to the world in an unmediated and very direct way, something that we are not often encouraged to do, but that is hugely rewarding and illuminating. The simplicity of the materials is a fundamental part of this creative process. Artist and art historian Deanna Petherbridge suggests that, '... drawings' primary role of invention (is enabled) by employing simple means'. The simpler the means, the more infinite the varieties are for us to explore and experiment with.

Different materials have different characters, potentials and limitations, therefore when you experiment with them and find different ways of combining them, they can lead to chance discoveries and present new possibilities and ways of responding to the world around you.

Many artists have used the limitation of materials to provoke new ideas or ways of working. Early on in her career, Georgia O'Keeffe limited herself to using just charcoal. She decided that until she reached a point when she absolutely could not express what she wanted to with only black and white, she would not use anything else. This limitation enabled her to explore all the infinite variations of mark, tone, texture, contrast, composition and transparency that were possible with charcoal alone and led her to develop her artistic voice in a way that was to be fundamental to her later work.

Lucian Freud, on the other hand, changed materials in order to prevent himself from making drawings that were too slick: as soon as he became too skilled at using one material he would discard it, 'like a blunt pencil', and find a new material that presented new challenges. During the 1930s, Joan Miró was so keen to experiment with chance marks made by different materials that he created a whole series of drawings initiated by spilling blackberry jam!

↓ Edgar Degas (1834-1917), Jockey on Horseback,
crayon on paper

Time

It can be very tempting to put off drawing until you have more time, no interruptions or until it feels like the right moment. There is no right moment, and it is always better to make a two-minute drawing today rather than hope to make a two-hour drawing tomorrow.

I am not suggesting that you never spend more than a few minutes on a drawing, but rather that time limitations can help you to get started. Try to get into the habit of fitting in time to draw even when you are busy. And if you are planning to make more sustained works it is a good idea to warm up with some quick drawings before you begin. There will always be other more pressing things that you have to do, but choose to pause and forget about everything else and just focus on looking and drawing, even if it is only for a few minutes.

When you are warming up, it is useful to use a timer to limit the amount of time that you spend on each drawing. Although this doesn't sound very spontaneous, it can actually free you from your own thoughts and inhibitions and allow you to be more intuitive and involved in looking and the physical act of drawing. It is amazing how long 2 minutes can feel and how much you can do in this short amount of time. What's more, time limits can stop you falling into the trap of wanting to make a perfect drawing and to spend hours trying to do this. You will find that when you have less time and are forced to work swiftly, with intense focus, you will make a more lively and interesting drawing. Think less and look more.

Finally, when you are drawing for short bursts

'Daily drawing is the best calisthenics one can have.'

Saul Steinberg, 1914–1999

of time, you don't have a moment to worry about whether you are any good or not, you just have to focus on looking! This can be very liberating if you are inclined to be self-critical. Make lots of drawings and don't worry if they are not all masterpieces, the chances are that a few of them will have something captivating about them. Matisse used to say, 'The 13th drawing is the one!'

→   Saul Steinberg, Untitled, 1949, ink on paper, 37.1 x 59.1cm

What to draw

Sometimes the biggest barrier to starting to draw is deciding what to draw. Although there may be occasions when you are fortunate enough to have your sketchbook with you when you see a blue whale or some other extraordinary sight, most of the time the best approach is to embrace the ordinary and the everyday. It is said that during the year that van Gogh lived and worked in a flat in Paris, he used to be exhilarated by what he could see from his window. He would spend days drawing directly onto the walls the scenes that he saw on the bustling street below. Matisse made some of his greatest creative breakthroughs making multiple drawings of a coffee pot, an orange, a particularly beloved chair and other objects that he had in his home and studio. So we have no excuse – grab a banana from the fruit bowl and start drawing!

Some other ideas for things to draw, in no particular order:
A cactus or other pot plant
Some fruit or vegetables
Your shoes or other items of clothing
The view from your window
A friend or a member of your family
Your pet, if you have one, or wild birds or animals
The interior of the room you are sitting in
The landscape or cityscape
A picture from a favourite art book or a treasured postcard
A fish or crustacean from the fishmonger or meat from the butcher
A jug or pot or something that inspires you from the kitchen cupboard
Your breakfast
A chair
The unmade bed
Your feet
Your hand
Whatever is sitting on the table in front of you
Piles of books
Twigs, stones, leaves, shells or bones
Clouds in the sky
Your reflection in a mirror

'I'm never inhibited
by working from life.
On the contrary,
I feel more free.'

Lucian Freud

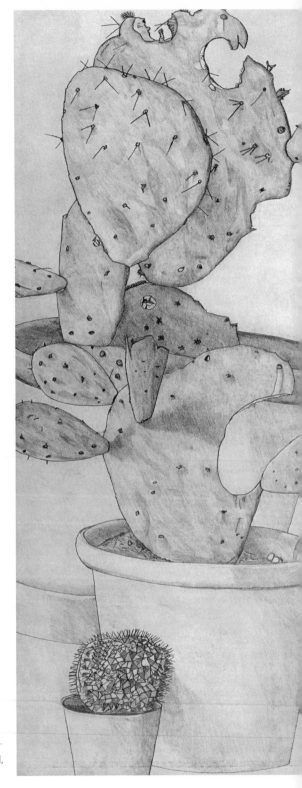

Where to draw

Although there is plenty to draw in and around your own home, drawing out and about can be very rewarding and full of surprises. If you are not in the habit of carrying your sketchbook, try to always take it with you when you head out of the door – you never know what you might see! Unexpected places and people might inspire you – sitting on a bus looking at your fellow passengers, walking through a street market or lying on the ground looking at the sky – there is no right or wrong place to draw. You may find it off-putting if people come and look over your shoulder while you are drawing in public places, but the more you do it the less distracting you will find this, and you might even inspire someone else to head out into the world with their sketchbook! If you are not used to drawing out and about it can be hard to know where to begin, so for those of you feeling a little overwhelmed by the idea, here are some suggestions:

Train stations and airports
Galleries and museums
Streets and squares
Markets
Zoos, wildlife parks or aquariums
Theatres and concert halls
On the train or bus
Farms, fields and open countryside
Woodland
River banks and bridges in the city or the countryside
The view from a plane, train or bus window
The interior or exterior of buildings
Public parks or gardens
Cafés, bars and restaurants

CHARCOAL

The fluidity and tonal possibilities of charcoal make it one of the most precious mediums available for searching, feeling and finding your way to the marks that best describe what you see or think. What's more, the lines made with charcoal can easily be erased, giving it the ability to transform seamlessly from one form to another, leaving only the faintest trace of the lost marks. Through charcoal the genesis of an idea can take form, can be worked through, and in short, can be brought to life. And because of its capacity for making large, flowing marks it is perfectly suited for drawing on a large scale, allowing you to use your whole body to draw across walls, canvas or paper. It is a very inexpensive, direct and physical material to use, being simply a piece of charred wood held in your hand.

According to Pliny the Elder, the story of painting and drawing began in ancient Greece with a primitive piece of charcoal. He tells of how a young Corinthian woman snatched up a burnt stick from the fireplace and traced on the wall the outline of her lover's profile cast by the light of a candle. We now know that some of the first drawings were indeed made with charcoal, but much earlier – up to 40,000 years ago – some extraordinary examples of which can be found in the Chauvet Cave in the Ardèche, France.

The cave's many chambers contain drawings and paintings that are twice as old as any previously ever found. One of the most astonishing sequences, the Panel of Horses, is drawn entirely in charcoal. It lies deep in the

'Charcoal is always reckoned to be the drawing medium closest to painting.'

Maggi Hambling, b. 1945

Chauvet Cave within the Hillaire Chamber. Images stream across 30 feet of undulating wall: aurochs, horses, rhinoceroses, cave lions, cave bears, bison and reindeer jostle for space, all in seemingly endless movement. They are quite alive despite the tens of thousands of years that have passed since the prehistoric artists applied the charcoal to the wall's surface.

And they are not mere outlines. The artists who have drawn these animals have used several techniques to bring them vividly to life, smudging the charcoal to create shadows, scraping and engraving the rock's surface with flint to create light, turning the charcoal into a paste, possibly by grinding it and then mixing it with spit, and even rubbing the charcoal with the wall's clay surface to create variations of colour and hue. The simplicity of the material seems to have enhanced the artists' inventiveness as opposed to diminishing it.

One of the many surprising things that these drawings reveal is that the artists who made them were not so different from us, that their experience of creating art was not unlike ours. They show us that prehistoric man was capable of imagining, thinking, reasoning and communicating with pictures and symbols, and therefore that the human brain was functioning in the same way then as it does now. Charcoal is a material that connects us directly to the experience of these ancient relatives.

For me, the most magical thing about them is that they were all drawn from memory. The details of behaviour, anatomy and movement of each species of animal were intensely observed and committed to memory before being carried in the mind's eye of each artist into the dark caves to be transferred onto its walls.

The charcoal that was used in Chauvet was made in situ in hearths close to where the drawings were executed. Remains of these hearths have been found, surrounded by fragments of charcoal. Analyses of these samples show that they were made from Scots pine and are around 32,000 years old.

Charcoal is made when wood is burnt without oxygen. Over the centuries it has continued to be made in a similar way. The fourteenth-century artist Cennino Cennini advises in *Il Libre dell'arte* (*The Craftsman's Handbook*) that to make 'perfect and slender coals for drawing' one must tie up willow sticks in bunches, put them in an airtight casserole, 'then go to the baker's in the evening, after he has stopped work, and put this casserole into the oven, let it stay there until morning and see whether these coals are well roasted and good and black'. Today, charcoal is made in a similar way. Sticks of wood are packed into an airtight container and then cooked for ten hours.

↓   Panel of Horses and a Woolly Rhinoceros,
Hillaire Chamber, Chauvet Cave, Charcoal and
Engraving, 32,000-30,000 BC. Artist: Art of the
Upper Paleolithic

Historically, the soft woods of vine and willow are favoured because of their smooth, rather than scratchy, quality and because their slender and straight shape make them perfect to draw with. Out of the nearly 400 species of willow trees and shrubs, the varieties most commonly used for making charcoal are the *Salix caprea*, or goat willow, and *Salix viminalis*, also known as basket willow, osier, sally or sallow. The English writer John Evelyn described it in *Sylva, or A Discourse on Forest-Trees and the Propagation of Timber*, a book that was published in 1664 and is still thought of as one of the most influential texts on forestry ever written:

'Sallow... is the most easy and accommodate for painters' scriblets to design their work, and first sketches on paper...'

These types of willow have been cultivated in Britain since ancient times and were used by the Vikings to weave various containers. They called it 'viker' which in Old English became 'wican', meaning 'to bend'. Willow is coppiced so that it grows in clumps of thin shoots that reach up to 8 feet tall (2 metres) but are as thin as twigs. These rods are harvested in the wintertime, when the leaves have fallen.

But as the pine charcoal found in the Chauvet Cave shows us, many other woods make an equally good drawing medium. Once, when I went to Ireland to draw for two weeks, my art materials went missing en route. While walking

'There may be a vague sense of what you're going to draw, but things occur during the process.'

William Kentridge, b. 1955

along the windswept lanes, I was delighted to find some burnt gorse bushes. I took the blackest bits that I could find back to the studio and discovered that not only could I draw with them, but that I actually enjoyed using them more than my shop-bought charcoal as they made a lovely soft, brown-black mark.

Likewise, there are no fixed rules for how you should use charcoal. In fact, it seems that this cheap and readily available material is the one that artists have felt most free to experiment with since the beginning. Crushed, rubbed, drawn, used dry or wet, it has long been the means for developing new languages of drawing and for pushing the boundaries of representation.

When Matisse was working out a series of large-scale drawings for the Chapel of the Rosary in Vence, France, he used charcoal attached to a long stick to draw directly onto the wall of his studio. In this way, the studio became a large canvas and living work of art,

← Paul Gauguin (1848-1903), Heads of Tahitian Women, Frontal and Profile Views, 1891-93, charcoal with brush and water on paper

41

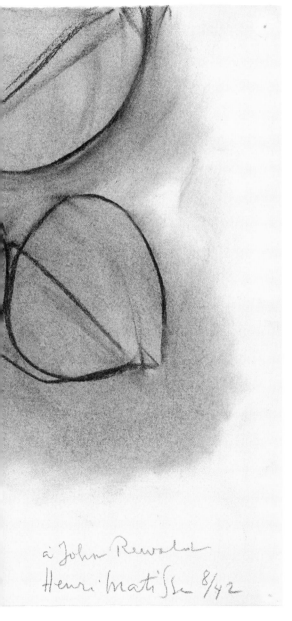

'One must always keep one's eyes, one's feeling, fresh, one must follow one's instincts.'

Henri Matisse, 1869–1954

not unlike the cave of Chauvet. This method of drawing subsequently allowed him to maintain a playful and experimental spirit in his work right until the very end of his life.

The South African artist William Kentridge has taken charcoal into new territories by creating large moving drawings using stop motion animation. Instead of completely erasing previous marks, the charcoal leaves its trace as the drawings transform from one frame to another. He seems to delight in the imperfection of the material, and this gives his films a raw energy that could not be created by more sophisticated materials or technology.

Despite the development of various new art materials, charcoal has remained irreplaceable because of its purity, authenticity and directness. It can give free reign to the artist's imagination and vision and a direct connection from mind to hand that is unchanged since it was first used by prehistoric man.

← Henri Matisse (1869-1954), Branch of a Judas Tree, 1942, charcoal on paper, 26.3 x 40.3cm

Charcoal techniques

Making dark and light marks
You can create dark or light marks by varying the pressure that you use.

Using the side of the charcoal to draw
You can make textured, wide, soft marks or cover large areas with the side of charcoal. It can easily be broken into shorter pieces to do this.

Various marks that can be made
Charcoal is very flexible, so experiment with the marks it can make; choppy, flowing, jagged, opaque or transparent etc.

Water washes (see Gauguin page 40)
You can create soft washes by applying water with a brush over your charcoal marks.

Crushing charcoal

Using crushed charcoal can create a beautiful variety of marks and textures. Place a stick of charcoal on a flat surface and crush using the side of a pencil or brush. The surface you use will get dirty, so you may want to cover it with newspaper first.

Using crushed charcoal

When the charcoal is evenly crushed, push into a cup or jam jar before gradually adding a little water, and a couple of drops of gum arabic if you have any. Then apply to paper with a brush, making it lighter or darker, by adding more or less water.

Creating a ground of charcoal and drawing into it

Using the side of a piece of charcoal, cover the paper with charcoal. You can rub the paper with your hand or kitchen paper to make the ground more even in tone. You can then work into this mid-tone ground using an eraser to draw light marks, and charcoal to draw in dark marks.

Fixing – important when using a sketchbook

Charcoal smudges easily, so when you have finished your drawing, take it outside and spray it with fixative. Avoid breathing in the fixative or using it in an unventilated space.

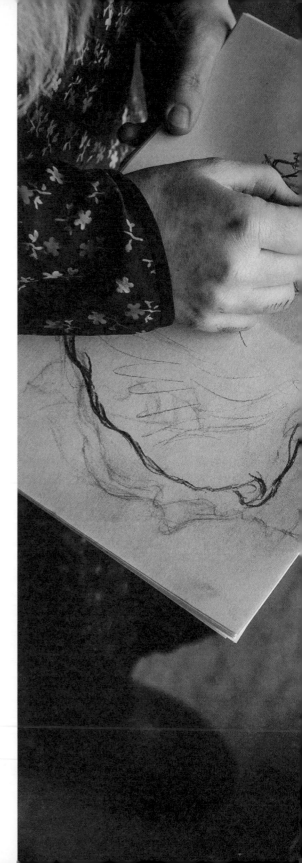

Charcoal
drawing
sessions

home
28.7.2020

Drawing session 1

Warming up: *2 minutes* Choose your subject, try to let all other thoughts fall away and focus on looking. Draw swiftly, using different pressures and marks to describe what you see. Let the lines flow to the edges of the page. Take up as much space as you need. Write the place and date. Fix.

Drawing session 2

Using the side of the charcoal: *5 minutes* Snap the charcoal into a 2.5cm (1-in) long piece. Lay it flat on the paper and draw using the side only. Try to think about the different tones of light and dark that you can see, pressing harder or more softly to describe them. Try to draw to the edges of your page. Write the place and date. Fix.

home 8.8.2020

Memory drawing: *4 minutes* Choose your subject. Look at it for 2 minutes without drawing. Just concentrate on looking and not thinking. Then, with the charcoal, draw from memory for 2 minutes without looking at your subject at all. Write the place and date. Fix.

Second memory drawing: *4 minutes* Shift your gaze, choose your subject, and again look for 2 minutes without drawing. During this time look at the overall shapes. Then draw from memory for 2 minutes, again without looking. Were you able to remember more in your second memory drawing? Write the place and date. Fix.

Drawing with light: *5 minutes* Cover the double-page spread in charcoal to make an even grey ground. Then draw your subject, lightening with an eraser and darkening with charcoal. It might help to work out where you can see the darkest and lightest points before you start to draw. Write the place and date. Fix.

Drawing session 5

Transparency and Opacity: *8 minutes* Using the charcoal, make four drawings, one on top of the other,
erasing the previous one before you start the next one. Try to draw across the whole double-page spread,
taking as much space as you need. First choose your subject, draw for 2 minutes, rub out this drawing then
move around your subject and make the next drawing. And repeat, drawing for 2 minutes each time and then
erasing the drawing before starting the next one, until the last drawing, which you will leave – this one will be
an accumulation of all four drawings (see page 48). Write the place and date. Fix.

Charcoal Washes: *5 minutes* Make a swift 2-minute line drawing of your subject, then look closely at where the shadows and tonal shifts are and with a jam jar of water and a brush, brush water into charcoal to make washes of grey and to soften charcoal marks. Write the place and date.

GRAPHITE

It is said that in Western Greenland the Inuit collect pebbles of graphite from dry brooks while travelling inland during the summer months. They carry this precious mineral with them through the dark winter, and then in the springtime take it with them to the coast for the annual hunt. Before setting off, they use the graphite to draw dark lines on their bleached paddles. They draw an image of Alinnaq, a deity associated with the moon, to ask him for help and good fortune in their hunt. The graphite marks are resistant to the arctic waters and so in this way they are able to take their deity with them on their perilous journey.

This is an extraordinary example of how graphite gives you the freedom to draw anything anywhere. When graphite was first discovered in England, in Cumbria, around 1500, it is said that the local people used the graphite to mark their sheep, which would also suggest that graphite can draw on just about anything! The exact truth about how the mines where found has been somewhat lost in the mists of time, but it is generally believed that it was found by a shepherd while tending his sheep on the mountains of Borrowdale. A large tree, some say an oak, some say an ash, had been blown down in a storm, and something glittering on the roots of the tree caught the shepherd's eye and so wadd, as it was known locally, was found.

At the time it was Europe's most valuable graphite mine. Queen Elizabeth I ordered a Company of Mines Royal to be set up there and it was protected day and night by armed guards. At first, the mineral was used mainly for

↑ Graham Sutherland OM (1903-1980), Sketchbook
I. Hilly landscape with a small, apparently ruined hut
or barn in the centre and the profile of a head on
the left 1935–6

ammunition, but gradually the pure, soft graphite became more sought-after as a drawing material, highly valued for its ability to make a dark, opaque mark that could be erased easily. It was exported to artists in Italy, France, Flanders and beyond. In these heady years, England had a near monopoly on the pencil industry.

But then France was cut off from this supply during the Napoleonic Wars, and in 1794 the French Minister of War, Lazare Carnot, challenged the people of France to invent an alternative worthy of her great artists. In just eight days, Nicholas Conté created a pencil that contained graphite made from powdered low-quality graphite (that could be sourced in France) mixed with clay. This meant that the graphite could be graded into different degrees of softness and hardness. The harder the pencil, the more clay it contained, and therefore was marked 'H' for hardness. The softer the pencil,

the less clay it contained, and was marked 'B' for blackness of mark (and so the softest pencil was called 9B and the hardest 9H).

At the end of the 1700s, the supply of graphite at the Borrowdale mine started to dwindle, and those in search of pure graphite needed to start looking further afield. It was not found until 1847 when an intrepid French explorer and trader called Jean-Pierre Alibert (1820–1905), who was panning for gold in a river in Siberia, noticed a strange and silvery pebble in the water. Believing it to be graphite, he decided to divert his entire expedition 430 kilometres to follow the river to its source. This took him 2,000 metres above sea level into a mountain range near the Chinese border. He was rewarded for his efforts, as here he found a rich and plentiful seam of graphite. Nowadays, graphite is mainly mined in China, India, Brazil, North Korea and Canada.

↑ John Constable (1776-1837), A baby (possibly Maria Louisa Constable), 1819, pencil on paper

Graphite is an allotrope of carbon. Pure carbon has three allotropes, or forms: diamond, graphite and buckminster fullerenes (or 'buckyballs') named after Buckminster Fuller. It is formed from atoms in layers and it is these layers that easily slip off the graphite onto the paper and leave a black mark. It was established as a mineral in 1779, and it was not until a century later that it was named 'graphite', after the Greek word 'graphein', meaning 'to draw' or 'to write'. Until then, it had been called many things, incuding plumbago, English antimony and Flemish stone (because it came to Southern Europe via Belgium and the Netherlands).

It continues to be one of the most perfect drawing materials. Not only because of the beautiful marks it makes, but also because it is portable and can be used in all weathers, even in the Arctic. (It was also a favourite with Russian astronauts because it works in zero gravity.)

'Do not fail, as you go on, to draw something every day, for no matter how little it is it will be well worth while, and will do you a world of good.'
Cennino Cennini, c. 1360–1427

↑   Maggi Hambling (b. 1945) Man on Bus, 1963,
ink on paper

The artist Mervyn Peake was devoted to graphite, in particular for its ability to create 'the frailest of grey to the black of the tomb'. Although some artists prefer to use graphite in the form of pencils, I am more drawn to using it in lumps and sticks because in these forms they make such wonderful broad and suggestive marks and can be used to build up silvery layers of mid-tone to draw into. When holding the graphite in my hand I am reminded of its elemental source – from deep inside a mountain or rolled along a riverbed – and this gives me a strong feeling of freedom, to draw whatever I see, wherever I am.

'Each time you address yourself to a little bit of paper to try and make a drawing of something it must be an experiment. Otherwise it won't have any life to it.'

Maggi Hambling, b. 1945

→ David Jones, 1895-1974 Study of wolves c.1942

Graphite techniques

Breaking graphite stick and drawing with the side
You can break the graphite stick to whatever size feels most comfortable to draw with. Much like charcoal, you can then draw with the side to make broad, textured marks and to cover large areas.

Varying your mark
With a graphite stick, you can make precise dark marks, soft marks, smudges, areas of very dark shadow or broad areas of texture. Try to explore all of the variations of marks you can make when you draw.

Creating a mid-tone ground with graphite

Using the side of the graphite stick, cover the page evenly with a mid-tone ground, ie. darker than the paper but lighter than the darkest mark you can make.

Drawing and erasing into the graphite ground

You can draw both light and dark marks into a mid-tone ground to create more depth and sense of form. Use an eraser to draw areas of light and graphite to draw lines and areas of darkness.

Smudging with fingers and hand

You can smudge, smear and smooth out graphite marks with your fingers and the palm of your hand. Don't be afraid to get your hands dirty!

Pressing hard and pressing softly

Explore the whole range of tones that you can make with graphite simply by varying the pressure that you use. You can create the deepest black to the most delicate grey.

Graphite washes

Like charcoal, you can create delicate washes by working into your graphite marks with a brush and water.

Drawing close and drawing far away

Anchor your drawing by describing something that is close to you: part of a building, a tree or even your own foot. You can draw things that are further away from you in relation to your 'anchor' and create a sense of depth.

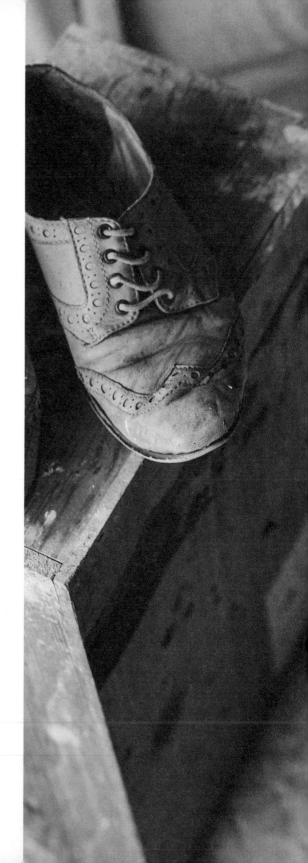

Graphite
drawing
sessions

Drawing with your left hand (or your right hand if you are left-handed): *2 minutes*
Choose your subject, then draw for 2 minutes, with your non-writing hand. Try to
use the whole page, embrace not being in control and let the lines flow. Write the
place and date.

Draw your own socks or shoes: *8 minutes* If you are ever feeling unsure what to draw, you can always find something in your wardrobe that has an interesting material, shape or pattern. The main focus of this drawing is varying your mark to describe what you are looking at. Use both the tip and side of the pencil or graphite stick. Fill the page. Write the place and date.

Drawing from the ground up: *5 minutes* This helps to situate yourself in a space and in your drawing, ie. exactly where were you standing when you drew that tree, person or building? You can do this drawing inside or outside with either pencil or graphite stick. Start the drawing looking down and draw from the ground up. I would encourage you to put your feet in, even it it's just your toes. This will help to anchor your drawing – where you are standing is the fixed point and you can navigate from there. You may want to turn your sketchbook 90° so that you have a more vertical space. Write the place and date.

Drawing a weed: *10 minutes* Find a weed – any weed will do. Either draw it in situ or bring it home and place it in a glass of water. I find plants easier to draw if there is a blank piece of paper or a wall behind them. Your drawing can take up as much space as you need, but try to draw across both pages and amplify rather than diminish the scale of your drawing. Write the place and date.

Night drawing: *2 minutes* This is a method of automatic drawing invented by the Surrealists. It can be done indoors, but is more interesting to do outside. Dusk is a good time to begin drawing as the light will gradually fade as you draw, creating more pronounced tonal areas and less detail. Decide where you are going to look, and spend a moment observing where the darkest and lightest areas are. Try using the side of the graphite stick to draw. Start to draw and focus on experimenting with making marks from the blackest black to delicate light grey. Write the place and date.

Drawing session 5b
Second night drawing: *2 minutes* You have warmed up now. Start by looking up and draw from the sky down to the ground, it doesn't matter if you don't manage to fit the horizon into the bottom of the page. Write the place and date.

Drawing near and far using either a pencil or graphite stick: *10 minutes* I recommend doing this outside, but you can also do it inside. Using the whole double page spread, first draw the thing that is closest to you, to anchor your drawing. Then gradually draw the things that are futher away from you, until you get to the edges of the page. It doesn't matter how much you fit in, just try to capture the larger scale of things that are close to you and the smaller scale of things that are far away. Write the place and date.

COLOUR CRAYONS

What could be more delightful and delicious than drawing with pure colour? For many of us, crayons have very happy associations of drawing freely and naturally as a child. But to dismiss crayons as child's play would be to miss out on a great pleasure for no good reason. Valued for their unique texture, they are a wonderful material that allow you to build up large areas of colour, to play off one vibrant hue against another, to layer colours, to draw thick opaque lines or delicate transparent lines and to use as a resist in water-based drawings.

Alongside charcoal, crayons were one of the first things that humans ever drew with. Prehistoric man used naturally occuring crayons of iron oxide red, manganese dioxide black and other earth colours. Lumps of these could be found in certain areas and dug out of the ground, and then cut or sharpened to serve as drawing materials. Cennino Cennini recollects being taken by his father, as a child, to see where these coloured earths were found at Colle di Val d'Elsa, 'Upon reaching a little valley, a very wild steep place, scraping the steep with a spade, I beheld seas of many kinds of colour.'

But crayons as we know them now – pigment bound with wax or oil – started to become popular in the nineteenth century when they began to be improved and produced for lithography. This new printmaking process was invented between 1796 and 1799 by an unknown Bavarian playwright called Alois

'Colour has its own existence; it possesses a beauty of its own.'

Henri Matisse, 1869–1954

Senefelder, who accidentally discovered that by writing with a greasy crayon on limestone he could, at very little cost, print an almost unlimited number of his theatrical works. The lithography process went on to be used widely to reproduce drawings and text, as well as becoming a means of artistic invention for many of the great artists of this period.

Franciso de Goya first experimented with lithography in 1819 in Madrid, but it was later during his final years, living in exile in Bordeaux, that he made his most extraordinary and inventive lithographs. The painter Antonio de Brugada, his companion and fellow *Madrileño*, described him at work:

'The artist worked at his lithographs on his easel, the stone placed like a canvas. He handled the crayons like paintbrushes and never sharpened them. He remained standing, walking backward and forward from moment to moment to judge the effect. He usually covered the whole stone with a uniform grey tint, and then removed the areas that were to be light with a scraper; here a head, a figure, there a horse, a bull. The crayon was then brought back into play to reinforce the shadows and accents, or to indicate figures and give them a sense of movement...'

Goya also used the lithographic crayon, which was mainly black, to draw on paper, particularly in his final two albums. The artist seems to have taken great pleasure in the rough and textured quality of the wax crayon. In one drawing, he portrays an old man with a great head of hair and beard moving forward with the aid of walking sticks. He entitled it: '*Aun aprendo*', 'I am still learning', and it is thought to be a self-portrait referring to the fact that he was still learning new skills and experimenting with new materials in his late seventies.

Henri de Toulouse-Lautrec (1864–1901) also used these crayons for drawing on both paper and stone, switching between the two with ease, to create his well-known free and grainy line.

Elsewhere, in Paris, van Gogh was making his own very simple but effective crayons. His friend, the Scottish artist Archibald Standish Hartrick, described in his memoirs how van Gogh made them: 'He would get hold of candle ends and he would melt them down in a metal spoon and he liked to use either red scarlet or blue powder and that gave him a big chunk of wax crayon that he carried in his pocket and if van Gogh saw something that excited him... he would feel in his pocket for one of these balls (of crayon) and he would automatically start drawing... He would draw on anything to hand, an evening paper left

↓ Frank Auerbach (b.1931), Study for Primrose Hill,   →   Pablo Picasso (1881-1973), Bull and Toreador,
1978, wax crayon on paper   1957, coloured wax crayons on board

18.5.57.

Dr Eugen Lamb   Lucca.   Aug 73   GH.

← David Hockney, Dr Eugene Lamb, Lucca, 1973, coloured pencil on paper (23½ × 20 in)

lying on the table or a doily, anything, a scrap of paper. He would be absolutely absorbed, trying to record something that excited him.'

It was not until the twentieth century that artist-grade colour crayons and coloured pencils started to be made commercially. In the making, both the proportions of wax or oil, pigment, binding agents and additives vary from one brand to another. Paraffin wax is often chosen as the carrier of pigment because it has very good 'rub off', which means that it leaves a satisfying, pigment-rich mark when it is drawn across the paper. As a general rule, the best artist-grade pencils or crayons contain more high-quality pigment and less filler, and therefore produce a much more intense and pure colour. However, saying this, I enjoy using Crayola crayons just as much as the more specialised and expensive ones. Possibly because they are less inhibiting.

Crayola is the most famous maker of crayons in America. The company was founded in 1885 and sends an astonishing 13.5 million crayons out into the world every day from its vast factory in Easton, Pennsylvania. Here, huge silos of paraffin wax are heated and moved into kettles, where they are mixed with powdered pigment and other additives. The coloured paraffin mixtures are then poured into moulds, where they are pushed through crayon-shaped cavities and sent off for labelling. They have an array of enticing names that make you want to get crayoning the rainbow immediately: dandelion, indigo, violet, yellow green, apricot, scarlet, carnation pink, cerulean, blue green... The list goes on.

Crayons, with their bright and varied range of

'Drawing makes you see things clearer, and clearer and clearer still until your eyes ache...'

David Hockney, b 1937

colours and waxy, textured mark, seem to invite creative freedom and artistic experiment, possibly because they lie somewhat outside the 'fine art' history. The Belgian artist James Ensor often used waxy coloured crayons in conjunction with dry crayons, chalk, ink, paint or whatever he had to create highly coloured and complex drawings. For Sonia Delaunay, coloured pencils provided an immediate and dynamic means of creating preliminary drawings for textile and cover designs. Perhaps she chose to use them because the rich texture and colour of crayons translate directly into the pure colour and feel of dyed cloth.

Henry Moore often drew with a white wax crayon, building up a series of criss-crossing lines, a method he called 'section line drawing', to create almost sculptural forms. He also combined wax crayon with other materials, using it as a water-resistant medium with ink or watercolour. In particular, in his shelter drawings (page 154), he uses the wax crayon to create the light in these otherwise shadowy subterranean drawings.

Colour crayon techniques

**Drawing large areas
of opaque colour**
Experiment with how colours
affect each other by drawing
areas of opaque colour next
to each other. See how colour
opposites make each other 'pop'.
You will need to press quite hard
to create areas of deep colour.

Making dark and light lines
Vary the pressure that you use
to create dark or light marks.
Use the side of the crayon to
create broad, textured marks
and the tip of the crayon to
create clear, strong marks.

Making coloured grounds
Break off a piece of crayon about 2.5cm (1in) long and, using the side of the crayon, rub the whole surface of the page, until you have an even-coloured ground to draw into.

Layering colour
Using the side of the crayons, make transparent layers of colour and see how different colours behave when drawn on top of each other. This can create a great ground to draw into.

Colour
crayon
drawing
sessions

Cover the page with colour: *4 minutes* Cover the double-page spread with blocks of colour, try not to leave any of the white of the page visible. The colours can overlap and can be drawn in any order, vary the pressure that you use. Discover which colours contrast the most and how different colours affect each other when they are next to each other or overlap. Write the place and date.

Drawing session 2a

Drawing your hand: *2 minutes* Place your non-drawing hand next to your sketchbook. Choose one colour crayon and draw this hand with one continuous line. Draw right off the edge of the page. Try not to judge your drawing, just focus on capturing the main shapes of your hand. Write the place and date.

Drawing session 2b
Second hand drawing: *5 minutes* All drawing is tonal, even when using colour. Take two colours and use one as your light and one as your dark. Once again, place your non-drawing hand next to your sketchbook, varying the position from before. Work out where the main areas of light and dark are and draw your hand using these two colours. Try not to centre your drawing and don't worry if you draw over part of your previous drawing. Write the place and date.

Drawing session 3
Draw your own room: *10 minutes* If you're not sure which room to draw, choose the one that you spend
most time in. Use two or three colours: one as your light, one as your dark and one as your mid-tone. Draw
right to the edges of the double-page spread. Try to include the floor. Write the place and date.

108

Drawing session 4a
Self-portrait using two colours: *4 minutes* Sit in front of a mirror making sure that your face is well lit. Break off 2cm (1-in) long pieces of any two crayons and decide which will be your light and which will be your dark. Draw with the side of the crayons. Focus on where the areas of light and dark are. Write the place and date.

Drawing session 4b
Self-portrait using three colours: *6 minutes* Taking inspiration from Charlotte Salomon's self-portrait (see page 9), choose three colours, break off 2cm (1-in) long pieces and use both the side and the tip of the crayons. Use colour tonally, so decide which colour will be your light, which will be your dark and which will be your mid-tone. Try to draw off the top and bottom of the page. Write the place and date.

Drawing session 5a

Memory drawing: *2 minutes* Choose your subject. Look at it for 1 minute without drawing. Sometimes it can help to 'draw' in the air with your finger while you do this to help you work out how you will draw it, but the most important thing is to focus on looking at your subject. Then take a colour and draw from memory for 1 minute without looking at your subject at all. Write the place and date.

Drawing session 5b
Second memory drawing: *3 minutes* Shift your gaze, choose your subject and again look for 1 minute without drawing. During this time look at the overall shapes and at what is closest to you as well as what is far away. Take a colour and draw for 1 minute without looking. Then take a second colour, look at your subject and draw what you see over your 'memory' drawing for 1 minute. Compare the memory drawing with the 'looking' drawing. How much were you able to capture from memory? Write the place and date.

Coloured ground: *10 minutes* Take two contrasting coloured crayons, break off a piece of the lighter of the two and using the side, cover this double-page spread with a coloured ground. It doesn't have to be perfect. Then with the other crayon, draw your subject. You may need to press really hard to capture areas of darkness. Write the place and date.

INK

The word ink comes from the Greek 'enkauston', meaning 'to burn in', derived from the ancient Greek practice of encaustic, painting with hot wax and pigment. In Roman times, it became 'encaustum', which was the name of the purple-red ink that was used by emperors – it was made from crushed shellfish that became a liquid ink when heated. Making this ink for anyone other than the Emperor was punishable by death. The word eventually became 'enke' or 'inke' in Medieval English, and finally 'ink' in modern times. A challenging material to master, ink is nearly impossible to erase and suits being applied at speed and with confidence. Nevertheless, it has endured as an indispensable material for artists. I believe that this is because of the potential for ink drawings to retain something of the fugitive moment in which they were made and, to tell us in a direct way, something of the hand and mind that made them.

The celebrated Japanese artist Hokusai was a painter, printmaker and master of ink and wash drawing. He was also a maverick and an innovator, famously using 54 litres of ink and a hemp broom to make a colossal 20-metre long portrait of Daruma, the founder of Zen Buddhism, during the Tokyo Festival in 1804. Several years later, at the age of 51, he created the first of the 'Hokusai Manga', a series of quick lessons in simplified drawings. He described this first book as, 'Brush gone wild' and went on to make a total of 15 volumes, which collectively contain thousands of deft and beautifully observed brush and ink drawings of

everyday people, religious figures, birds, beasts, plants and the supernatural. These were very popular at the time and later inspired the manga comics of today. Hokusai continued to make an abundance of ground-breaking work until his death at 88. The following statement, made in his mid-seventies, gives a clear impression of his boundless creative energy and desire to learn:

'When I reach 80 I hope to make increasing progress; at 90 I will see the underlying principle of things... at 100 I will have achieved divine status as an artist and at 110, every dot and stroke will be alive.'

It also gives us an insight into what drove him, and what made his work so astonishing – his intention to make every mark vibrate with life. A reminder that the artist's intention is everything, it is what makes the difference between an exciting drawing and an unremarkable one.

Meanwhile in Spain, the artist Francisco Goya, a near contemporary of Hokusai, was also using ink to portray his times. In his albums of drawings, figures from all walks of life dance, march, fall, fight and fly across the page. He uses dry brush marks, flowing dark lines, light watery washes, darkly inked shadows, the stark white of the paper, dots and dashes of ink to bring each figure vividly to life.

In the first two albums Goya used Indian ink and fine foreign paper, but in the third album he starts to use oak gall ink on locally made paper. This was probably out of necessity as these drawings seem to have been made during the war years (1808–14) when the Spanish people fought against Napoleon Bonaparte's invading

> ## 'Because I now have such a broad, ample feeling for art and for life itself, of which art is the essence.'
>
> Vincent van Gogh

armies, a time when imported artist's materials would have been hard to come by in Madrid.

Historians suggest that ink was first invented by the Egyptians. The oldest known book written in ink is the Prisse D'avennes papyrus, which dates to 2600BC. The main body of this book is written with a very opaque mixture of lampblack, water and a binder (a sugar called gum arabic). Amazingly, this ink is perfectly stable over time, doesn't fade, is chemically neutral and is more or less the same as the artist's black ink that we use today. Another similar version of ink was invented in China 3,000 years later. This is also made with lampblack, which is simply soot mixed with water and a binder. It is called Chinese ink, but confusingly, is also known as Indian ink. An account from ancient China describes how the lampblack was collected from hundreds of small earthenware oil lamps enclosed in a bamboo screen, to keep the wind

'A line, an area of tone, is not really important because it records what you have seen, but because of what it will lead you on to see.'

John Berger, 1926–2017

out; every half an hour or so the workers would collect the soot from the lamp funnel using a feather.

For Chinese artist scholars, learning how to use ink was not so much a technique as a philosophy. Each of the myriad marks such as 'lo-pi' (the moment that the brush touches the paper), 'ts'un' (a raindrop-shaped stroke) and 'tsa-pi' (a rubbed-brush mark) had a distinct meaning. In this way, their drawings were not only a visual representation of the world but also had a poetic meaning that could be read by the viewer. The use of ink was highly ritualised both for writing and for drawing, so exotic ingredients such as crushed pearls, jasper and

rhinoceros horn were sometimes added, as well as perfumes such as cloves, honey and musk.

Other inks that have long been used by artists are oak gall ink and sepia ink.

Oak gall ink, also known as iron gall ink, was the most commonly used writing and drawing ink in Europe from around the fifth century until the nineteenth century and continues to be used by some artists today. When first applied it is blue-black, but over time it becomes a soft, velvety dark brown. It is made using the tannic acids found in oak galls, a nut-like growth that forms around wasp larvae when they are laid in the developing leaf buds of the oak tree. The oak gall is mixed with iron sulphate, water and gum arabic. It is a very stable ink that can last for well over a thousand years, but if there is an imbalance of ferrous ions it creates dark halos around the ink marks and can corrode holes through the paper or vellum that it is drawn upon.

Sepia ink has been used since ancient Greek times for both drawing and writing and was a favourite with Leonardo da Vinci. It is made from the ink sack of the cuttlefish, a type of cephalopod that squirts ink into the water when threatened by a predator. The temporary 'smoke screen' of ink gives the cuttlefish a chance to escape. The ink is made mainly from melanin and creates a warm-toned brown drawing medium that is permanent.

In European art of the nineteenth and twentieth centuries, brush or pen and ink drawings came to be associated with a more instinctive or primal way of working. Like

Bajan riñendo

Philip Guston

← Philip Guston (1913-1980), Preparatory drawing from 'In Memory of My Feelings', 1967, ink on paper

charcoal, ink has a directness and pureness that is valued by artists, particularly when trying to return to a point of origin.

Alexander Cozens created a blot method: a playful and unpredictable way of using ink that produced unexpected and suggestive marks that he would then develop into drawings. He wrote, 'To sketch in the common way, is to transfer ideas from the mind to the paper... to blot is to make varied spots and shapes with ink on paper, producing accidental forms without lines, from which ideas are presented to the mind'. And he recommended, 'For the surest means of producing a great variety of the smaller accidental shapes, the paper on which you are going to make the blot, may be crumpled up in the hand, then stretched out again.'

In 1953, Picasso made 180 ink drawings over the course of a couple of months, no doubt inspired on some level by the many ink drawings made by Goya in his albums.

Philip Guston also made hundreds of ink drawings while working through a transition from abstract to figurative art: 'I did literally hundreds and hundreds of drawings, mostly in brush and ink, and charcoal on paper. They were all over the walls and floors... my strongest sensation at that time was a feeling of needing to start again with the simplest means to clear the decks. The drawings that didn't work, and were just thrown away, were just lines. In the ones that were good the whole space was activated'.

Since its invention, artists have experimented with ink and pushed it to its limits; some even finding a spectrum of colours within its

'It is the bareness of drawing that I like. The act of drawing is what locates, suggests, discovers.'

Philip Guston, 1913–1980

blackness. Hans Jurgen Blames said, '... We have been experimenting with John's (John Berger) English ink. It can be coaxed into developing different colours if you add some sugar, salt. If you spit in it, some blue or red or velvet will appear in the grey wash between the lines'.

So I would encourage you to experiment and take risks with this lively material that rewards the brave! Not being very courageous myself I have often found it very intimidating, which is why I started using it for night drawing, then once freed from the fear of making a 'mistake' I allowed the ink to flow freely and discovered that only then does the ink come into its own. But if all fails you can take a page out of Louise Bourgeois' book: 'Razor blades and erasers are indispensable... You can rub anything out. Ink is permanent: actually not quite, because the best ink of all is the white ink that lets you cover and obliterate. If I want to erase something, I put on some white, the negative is more important that the positive'.

124

← William Kentridge
Drawing for 'Lulu', 2013
Indian ink and red pencil

Ink techniques

Ink washes
You can create ink washes simply by diluting the ink with water. Pour some ink into a jam jar and then add water until you have the lightness or darkness of wash that you want. You can also brush water over ink marks to create areas of tone.

Create different tones
Before you start to draw, it is a good idea to try out a few different dilutions of ink to see the range of tones that you can get from light to dark. Some inks are more opaque than others, so this will give you a chance to familiarise yourself with how your ink behaves.

Various marks that can be made
Brush and ink can create a great variety of marks: flowing, choppy, thin, thick, transparent, opaque, and so on. Try to vary your mark in order to describe the character, texture and shape of what you are drawing.

Loaded brush, dry brush
Brush and ink behaves very differently depending on how loaded the brush is. Try drawing with only a little ink on your brush to create very scratchy, textured marks and try drawing with the brush soaked in ink to create flowing marks and areas of tone.

Making your own still life

You may just want to place a couple of pebbles together or a vegetable or two or you may choose to make something more ambitious, it is up to you. Thomas Gainsborough used to build small landscapes in his studio to paint and draw from. He used broccoli to make trees, mirrors for water, pieces of coal for rocks and bits of stick or branch for foliage. It is important to place your chosen objects so that you can see them and the fall of light upon them without too many distractions. You can either place them on a table or surface and look down on them or place in front of something plain around eye level.

Layering one

With ink, you can make layers of marks to create depth and to describe the fall of light. It is best to start with a light wash (by diluting the ink with water) and layer the marks over the top, working from light to dark.

Layering two

If the first ink wash is very wet, any marks that you make on top of it will bleed – this can be an interesting way of working but if you don't want this to happen, let the first wash dry before you apply more marks. You can draw over ink washes either with the same lightness of wash as the first layer or with a darker ink wash or pure ink.

Drawing with a stick

Ink is a very flexible and simple material. You can apply it with anything from a quill, a pen, a brush or even your finger – each of these will give you a different degree of control over your medium. Try using a stick – you will need to dip it in the ink more often than a brush, but you will be rewarded with an interesting and often surprising mark.

Ink drawing sessions

Drawing fast: *2 minutes* You will need a brush and a jam jar of ink, a jam jar of water to dilute and kitchen paper (to soak up any excess or spilt ink/water.) Make a swift drawing of your chosen subject. Let your drawing take up as much of the double-page spread as necessary. Focus on the main shapes. Don't worry about detail. Write the place and date.

Drawing slow: *6 minutes* You will need a brush and a jam jar of ink, a jam jar of water to dilute and kitchen paper. Using layers of ink, make a longer drawing. Try using a light ink wash, a dark ink wash, as well as the white of the page and pure black ink to create a broad tonal range. Draw right to the edges of the double-page spread. Write the place and date.

Night drawing: *4 minutes* You will need a brush and a jam jar of ink, a jam jar of water to dilute and kitchen paper. Draw at dusk or night time. If you can't go outside, draw from your window. Let this drawing dry before turning the page. Write the place and date.

Drawing session 3b

Second night drawing 2: *4 minutes* You have now warmed up. Shift your gaze and focus on a different part of what you can see. Don't worry if it is too dark to see your drawing, this will only make it more exciting when you bring it into the light to see the result. Write the place and date.

Drawing wet into wet: *4 minutes* You will need a cloudy day for this! You need a brush and a jam jar of ink, a jam jar of water to dilute and kitchen paper. To begin, brush a wash of water over the double-page spread, then look up at the sky and select an area of clouds to focus on. It may help to have a jam jar lid with some diluted ink to use as well as pure ink. Start drawing and don't worry if the clouds change completely while you draw, just keep drawing and trying to capture what you see, as this will give your drawing a sense of movement. Let this drawing dry before you turn the page. Write the place and date.

Drawing session 4b
Second drawing wet into wet: *4 minutes* Focus on another part of the sky and make a second drawing. Clear your mind of other thoughts and just think about where the sky shifts from dark to light and how to describe the clouds closest to you as well as those further away. Write the place and date.

Build your own still life: *4 minutes* You will need a brush and a jam jar of ink, a jam jar of water to dilute and kitchen paper. Place your chosen subjects on the surface in front of you. Make sure they are well lit. Focus on the fall of light and the shadows that your objects cast as well as the objects themselves. Try to describe these with dark and light ink washes and pure ink. Write the place and date.

Drawing with found materials: *5 minutes* Find a stick and, with your jar of ink, use as a dipping pen and draw your chosen subject. Try to use the whole double-page spread and experiment with the different marks that you can make with this simple tool. Try to embrace not being in complete control. Write the place and date.

COLOURED PAPER

For some, the sight of a blank white page is exciting and full of possibility, while for others it can be daunting, to say the least. But there is no need to draw on a pristine piece of bright white paper, and in fact over the centuries artists have found many ways of avoiding just this. It is said that Turner used to draw and paint on the blue paper that sugar was traditionally wrapped in, Picasso was fond of cardboard and Michelangelo laboriously glued together small scraps of used paper to make what must have been a rather lumpy but characterful new sheet to draw on. When Louise Bourgeois was making her 'Insomnia Drawings', a series of doodles, drawings and notes that she made during a period of time when she couldn't sleep, she drew on manuscript paper, graph paper, blue letter paper, lined paper or whatever she could put her hands on in the middle of the night. For the British sculptor Barbara Hepworth, drawing was an important part of her process. She said, 'When I am making a drawing, I like to begin with a board which I have prepared with a definite texture and tone. I like to rub and scrape the surface as I might handle the surface of a sculpture'.

The most simple way to avoid the stark flatness of a white page is to apply a coloured or monochrome ground to the paper. This can be done by either brushing or sponging over the paper a translucent wash made of diluted acrylic, ink or watercolour. There are many reasons why drawing on tinted paper can be very rewarding. It removes some of the blankness and provides an existing texture, colour or tone for you to

'Drawings are thought feathers, they are ideas that I seize mid-flight and put down on paper.'

Louise Bourgeois, 1911–2010

and delicate version of parchment called vellum. Because of the lengthy process necessary to prepare these surfaces, they were extremely expensive and not always easy to come by. As a result, they were used very carefully and sparingly by artists, and the drawings made on them tended to be meticulously planned and highly finished.

When paper came onto the scene, it was much more affordable and readily available than vellum or parchment had ever been. As a result, artists had more freedom to experiment and to search out new ways of depicting the world. Drawing from life became more possible as artists could take the less precious paper out into the streets and into the landscape more easily and fleeting phenomena like movement, weather and natural light could all be explored more readily when not every drawing had to count. You only need to look at the 'brainstorming' sheets of Leonardo da Vinci to see the expressive and intellectual freedom that an affordable and durable surface like paper gave to artists.

These early adopters of paper were mainly using either ink, or silverpoint to draw with before the invention of the pencil. The paper did not have to be prepared in any way to draw with ink but artists often tinted the surface in order to provide a middle tone, or simply to make the sheet more attractive. Antonio Pisanello, for example, preferred to draw on paper prepared with a reddish-pink wash.

spark ideas off. The tinted ground provides a tone midway between light and dark so that you can quickly create the illusion of three dimensions and the fall of light. Rather than relying on the white of the paper itself, you can draw the light with an opaque white material such as chalk. Also, importantly, paper prepared in this way is suited to being used outside as the less dazzling surface doesn't blind you in bright sunlight.

The use of coloured grounds to draw on has gone hand in hand with the use of paper itself. Paper was the single most important reason for the flourishing of drawing from the 1400s onwards. Although it is easy to take it for granted that we draw on paper now, it was not until a blossoming printing industry brought about the mass production of paper that it became widely available to artists. Until the 1450s, artists had mainly drawn on parchment, made from sheep or goat skin, or a more refined

---

→ Louise Bourgeois, The Insomnia Drawings, 1994-95, ink and coloured pencil on paper (27.9 x 20.7cm)

'Be bold, have a go and risk your paper.'

Samuel van Hoogstraten, 1627–1678

Silverpoint, on the other hand, could only be used on a prepared ground. The paper had to be covered with a slightly abrasive surface so that when the soft metal of the silverpoint was drawn across it, a trace of silver was left, making a delicate mark that would tarnish and darken over time. To make a ground for silverpoint, a mixture of ground bone ash and a small amount of pigment are bound together with rabbit skin glue or an equivalent binder. Earth pigments such as red earth, yellow ochre or umber, as well as blue pigments are the most commonly used to tint the ground.

In Leonardo da Vinci's *Treatise on Painting* he advises artists to, 'Be sure to take with you a little book with pages prepared with bone meal, with a silverpoint briefly note the movement and actions of the bystanders and their groupings.'

One of the disadvantages of the silverpoint and prepared ground is that it is hard to erase the marks that you make. However, Leonardo sees this as a positive thing for it encourages you not to erase and correct but instead to move on to the next drawing, thus preserving the swift and spontaneous marks that you make. He writes that the pages of your sketchbook 'should be of coloured paper, so that you cannot rub your sketch out, but will have to change from an old page to a new when the old one is filled....'.

Another reason why these early draughtsmen rarely drew on white paper was because in the 1400s papermaking was still in its infancy in Europe. At this time, Venice was the main producer of paper as the city was home to a thriving textile industry, which provided a constant supply of scraps of linen and cotton that were mashed into a pulp and poured into paper-shaped moulds. The rags themselves were rarely pure white in colour, so the papermakers would adjust the hue by adding other coloured fabrics to the pulp. For example, if the paper was too yellow some blue coloured scraps of fabric would be introduced to neutralise the yellow tint. And by using scraps of cotton and linen dyed with indigo a paper of various blue hues could be made.

Thanks to trade with the rest of Europe and the East, indigo and other dye stuffs were readily available in Venice and, at this time, it was the only city in Europe producing blue paper. It became very popular with the Venetian artists of the day, possibly because it was so suited to exploring the play of light and dark in their shimmering city of water and reflected light. But soon its popularity spread and by

→ Leonardo da Vinci, (1452-1519) A horse in profile, and from the front, metalpoint on paper

154

'I draw the thing
into existence —
I can only think
through doing.'

Paula Rego, b. 1935

1510 the Nuremberg artist Albrect Durer
was enthusiastically using it, possibly having
discovered it on his travels through Italy.

Looking back at the history of coloured
grounds it seems to me that it is a story of
opening up the possibilities of paper, of giving
artists more freedom to combine materials,
colours and textures in new, and often painterly,
ways and to make marks without worrying
about losing the sacred whiteness of the page.
In this chapter, I encourage you to combine the
different materials introduced in this sketchbook
with the addition of white chalk. The following
pages have various coloured and monochrome
grounds for you draw into and to create your
own contrasts of texture, colour and light.

← Henry Moore (1898-1986), Shelter Drawing
1940, 289 × 273 mm, pencil, wax crayon, coloured
crayon, watercolour, pen and ink

Tinted paper techniques

Making coloured grounds with acrylic paint or ink

Ultramarine blue and earth coloured acrylics, such as yellow ochre and red or green earth, are useful colours for coloured grounds. Dilute about a teaspoon of acrylic paint of your chosen colour in half a jam jar of water, mix with a large brush (a hog brush or priming brush are good for this). Add more paint or water until you have the desired tint. Then brush evenly onto your paper. Similarly, to make a mid-tone ink ground, mix ink with water until you have a mid-tone wash, then brush evenly onto your paper.

Using earth pigments to create a ground

You can also use pieces of earth pigment, such as red earth, to create a coloured ground. Simply rub evenly all over the paper's surface. You can then rub your hand or a tissue across the surface to get a more even finish.

Coloured crayons on a coloured ground

You can experiment with opposite colours by drawing with crayons that contrast strongly with the coloured ground, making your line 'pop'.

Pencil and crayon

Combine monochrome and coloured drawing materials to create a variety of marks and textures. Try using graphite to describe structure and coloured crayons to describe areas of light and dark.

Experimenting with all the materials

See how you can combine the different materials that you have used so far, for example, try drawing with crayon over a charcoal ground or drawing with graphite and chalk over a light ink wash ground, adding colour with crayon, and so on. The possibilities are endless.

Chalk, pencil and ink wash

Using these materials, you can create the illusion of form and depth. You can use the pencil to draw the structure, the ink washes to describe the shadows and areas of darkness and the white chalk to pick out the areas of light.

Wax relief and ink

Choose a subject that has strong contrasts of light and dark. Draw with a white crayon or a light coloured crayon. You will need to make quite heavy opaque marks in order for them to be visible. Then brush ink over the whole page to see your drawing appear. You can use a rag to wipe away ink from your wax drawing to lighten.

Drawing with charcoal and chalk over an ink wash

Mix a mid-tone wash of ink and water and brush evenly over your paper. Once the ink wash is dry, choose a subject that has strong contrasts of light and dark and use the chalk to describe the lightest points and the charcoal to describe the shadows and the points of darkness.

Coloured paper drawing sessions

Drawing session 1
Drawing with light: *2 minutes* Choose your subject, and using a piece of chalk, let your lines flow across the page, and try to fill the double-page spread, varying the pressure you use to make stronger or lighter marks. Write the place and date.

Exploring colour relationships: *10 minutes* Try to choose a colour that contrasts strongly with your coloured ground so that you can experiment with how they affect one another. For example, using opposites such as green and red next to each other will make the green appear more green and the red more red. Choose your subject and draw, letting your lines flow across the page. Write the place and date.

Draw from the sky downwards: *5 minutes* Use a pencil and two colour crayons. When we draw we often focus on the horizon and centre it in the middle of our drawing, but it doesn't have to be so! A drawing can be much more dynamic if the horizon is near the top or near the bottom of your page. Start your drawing by looking up at what is above your head, draw from there down until you run out of space. You can use the pencil to describe the structure of what you are looking at and the crayons to describe areas of colour or tone. Write the place and date.

Drawing session 4

Wax relief and ink: *10 minutes* Using a white wax crayon, or the lightest colour you have, draw your subject. You will need to make heavy, deliberate and broad marks, rather than thin, light lines. Use as much of the double-page spread as you can. Once you feel that you have made a strong enough drawing of your subject, brush black ink over the whole page. If some parts of your drawing don't appear, then wipe away the ink with kitchen paper to reveal the wax marks. Write the place and date.

Drawing session 5
Charcoal and chalk on a mid-tone ground: *10 minutes* Once you have chosen your subject, look carefully at how the fall of light describes it, then using charcoal draw the shadows and use chalk to pick out the brightest points. Try to create a strong contrast between the mid-tone paper and the light and dark marks that you make on it. This will make your drawing 'pop' and appear more three dimensional. Write the place and date.

Self-portrait with pencil, ink wash and chalk on a coloured ground: *10 minutes* Find a mirror and sit comfortably in front of it, try to make sure that your face is fairly well lit either by natural or artificial light. You will need to place a jam jar of diluted ink, brush, pencil, eraser and some chalk within reach. I suggest that you use the pencil to find the form and structure and the ink wash to describe the areas of shadow. The chalk is there to pick out the brightest points, such as the bridge of your nose. Don't worry about detail, just try to capture what is most characteristic about your face. Write the place and date.

Use this page to try out different materials and the marks that you can make with them.

Credits